January

Julie Murray

Abdo
MONTHS
Kids

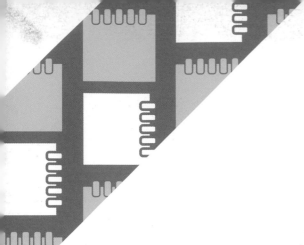

abdopublishing.com

Published by Abdo Kids, a division of ABDO, PO Box 398166, Minneapolis, Minnesota 55439.
Copyright © 2018 by Abdo Consulting Group, Inc. International copyrights reserved in all countries.
No part of this book may be reproduced in any form without written permission from the publisher.

Printed in the United States of America, North Mankato, Minnesota.

052017

092017

THIS BOOK CONTAINS
RECYCLED MATERIALS

Photo Credits: Getty Images, iStock, Shutterstock

Production Contributors: Teddy Borth, Jennie Forsberg, Grace Hansen

Design Contributors: Christina Doffing, Candice Keimig, Dorothy Toth

Publisher's Cataloging in Publication Data

Names: Murray, Julie, 1969-, author.

Title: January / by Julie Murray.

Description: Minneapolis, Minnesota : Abdo Kids, 2018 | Series: Months |
    Includes bibliographical references and index.

Identifiers: LCCN 2016962334 | ISBN 9781532100154 (lib. bdg.) |
    ISBN 9781532100840 (ebook) | ISBN 9781532101397 (Read-to-me ebook)

Subjects: LCSH: January (Month)--Juvenile literature. | Calendar--Juvenile literature.

Classification: DDC 398/.33--dc23

LC record available at http://lccn.loc.gov/2016962334

Table of Contents

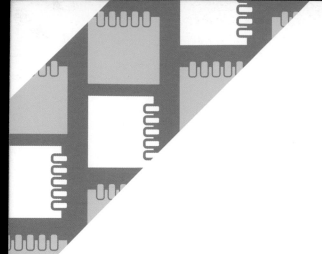

January

There are 12 months

in the year.

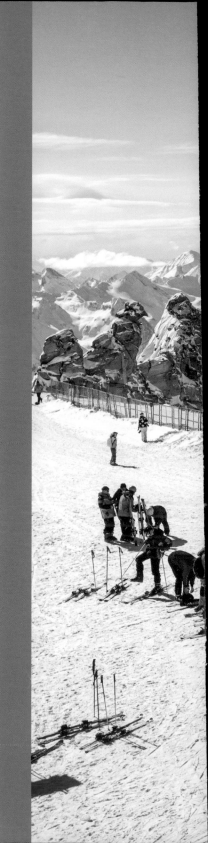

January

February

March

April

May

June

July

August

September

October

November

December

5

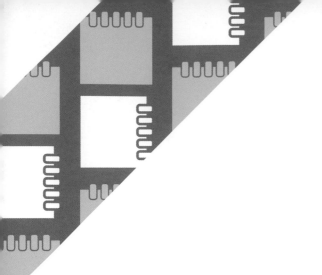

January is the 1st month.

It has 31 days.

January

1	2	3	4	5	6	7
8	9	10	11	12	13	14
15	16	17	18	19	20	21
22	23	24	25	26	27	28
29	30	31				

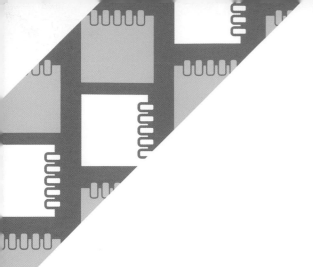

New Year's Day is the first day of the year. Pete blows the horn!

9

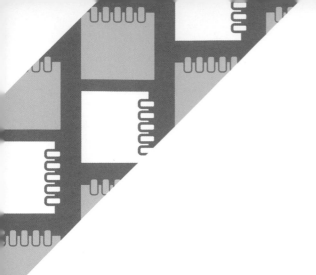

Martin Luther King Jr. Day is in January. It is the third Monday.

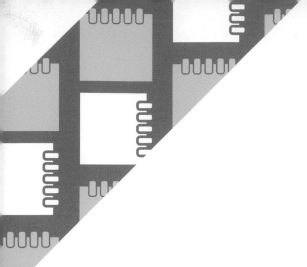

Benjamin Franklin's birthday is this month. He was born on January 17, 1706.

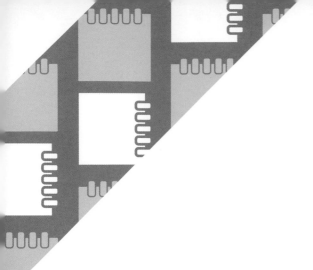

January can be cold. Tami wears a hat and mittens.

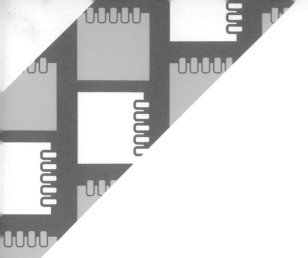

Max lives in Ohio. He enjoys the snow. He sleds with Claire.

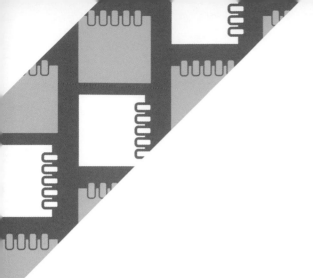

Sam builds a snowman.

Jake helps!

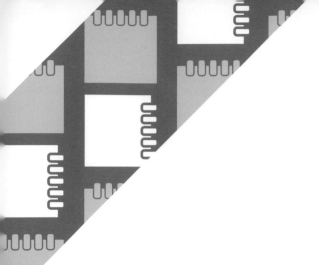

Ella lives in Iowa. She ice skates.

She loves January!

Fun Days in January

National Bird Day
January 5

National Hug Day
January 21

National Pie Day
January 23

National Peanut Butter Day
January 24

Glossary

Benjamin Franklin
one of the Founding Fathers of the
United States, as well as an author,
scientist, inventor, and more.

Martin Luther King Jr. Day
a day that celebrates MLK Jr. and
his fight for equal rights.

Index

abdokids.com

Use this code to log on to abdokids.com and access crafts, games, videos, and more!

Abdo Kids Code:
MJK0154